Treasury Holiday

THE WESLEYAN POETRY PROGRAM: VOLUME 53

Treasury Holiday

Thirty-four Fits for the
Opening of Fiscal Year 1968

by William Harmon

WESLEYAN UNIVERSITY PRESS
Middletown, Connecticut

Acknowledgement is gratefully made to The University of North Carolina Press, the publishers of *Sample Copy*, in which certain parts of this poem were first published in slightly different form, and to Doubleday & Company, the publishers of *Quickly Aging Here*, an anthology edited by Geof Hewitt, in which other parts were first published in slightly different form.

Hardbound: ISBN: 0-8195-2053-5

Paperback: ISBN: 0-8195-1053-x

Library of Congress catalog card number: 78-120263

Manufactured in the United States of America

First printing September, 1970; second printing October, 1970

Treasury Holiday

I am the Gross National Product
absorb & including all things all goods Fab with Borax
Kleenex Clorox Kotex Kodak & Ex-Lax
I contain the spectacular car-crash death of the movie star
    Jayne Mansfield
& the quiet death of John Masefield the word star equally
the Baby Ruth no less than the Crab Nebula
I do not distinguish or discriminate the murmuring
of pine & poison The gross the great the grand National
pure products the good doc said go crazy
Lord God of Hosts I am the Gross National Product of the
    United States of America & here celebrate the New Fiscal Year
this fourth of July in the Lord's anno
one thousand plus one thousand minus one hundred plus fifty plus
    ten plus five plus three ones
in Mod. Am. Eng. ALFA DELTA 11110110000
I am the grand central Brother Jonathan & Uncle Sam
red white & blue-black all
I am first second & third persons singular & plural nominative
    genitive accusative & focative
absorbing & subsuming all including Mister Fats Domino
Alexander Hamilton the handsome treasurer & Gaylord Wilshire
    & Sylvester Graham & Mary Baker Eddy
O national product composed of compositions of all sorts of sorts
melting pot mulligan mulligatawny & huge buildings
& I reject the government as such for the government as nonesuch
& I categorically deny education religion youth communication love
    industry poetry & all arts & sciences & games & nature & culture
all subordinated quite to one gross & national product in terms of
the lordly Long Green
money the only mother
money the only poetry

they say LSD in England pounds shillings pence O pounds of money
money the only gross national poem & noumenon
for it is a good thing to me including all things & by its intermediation
    making them all holy one & all
the cheap ugly vulgar things
& language
holy body of money the only poetry
O gross & National bills coins post stamps lard futures bonds
    vouchers gilt-edge blue-chip shares checks & military payment
    certificates & rapid-transit tokens

ii

Now he is the Declaration of Independence a poem beginning with
    the rhyme When in
Now he is the Constitution a poem beginning with the rhyme We the
Now the Gettysburg Address a poem beginning with the rhyme
    Four score

iii

Atheist in religion anarchist in politics analphabetist in literature &
    good in all things I am myself everywhere
geography includes me & holds me cabined in its bosom
& I transcend the gross chorography to go plumb across coughing
    oceans on great circles & rhumblines in acorns & up the sky
    in steel seeds
go crazy products incorporated now fourth of Julius year of Jesus
neither congruent to us absolutely but included entirely herein
I grant Frigg her day
& pledge allegiance to the telephone
In motherfucker we trust

Computer the Gem of the Xerox
I'm stuffed from sea to shining sea with an immaculate gamut of
      supermarkets & fanes of ALGOL laundromats & left- &
      right-wingers & bluegrass clowns in union suits & gypsy
      babbitts & popular music
advertising cones & locofoco engineers & Queequegs & bimetallist
      homosexuals & abstracted seraphim & every e pluribus &
      quaquaversal thing
America O holy poetry the only Mary the only money

iv

One thousand $(10^3$
plus nine hundreds $(10^2$
plus six tens $(10^1$
plus eight atom units $(10^0$
I contradict I contradict
counting bits counting click the poem money month numbers
a teller
dough of anonymous pleasure & body potlatch
I am your gross national poem phenomenon & do not think that
      large social institutions are at all evil in their supposed
      depersonalizing effect upon the spirit & dignity of man but good
good not only as a piece of mass made metal machinery is good
      but good even as a flower is good
a flea or tick is good
& that the 500 most gigantic megalocorporations catalogued
      annually in Fortune magazine make a lovely chronicle of
      knowledge & goodness for all men
that International Harvester & Coca Cola International & Rotary &
      Kiwanis & Lions International
International Telephone & Telegraph & International Business
      Machines are holy

are ordered in celestial hierarchies like seraphim cherubim thrones
    dominations virtues powers principalities archangels & angels
virgins martyrs fathers doctors metropolitans & patriarchs We
are the gross national enormous suburb

     v

They look forward with whole joy to the day when the entire
    country is paved
& every square cubit & parsec thereof graded & covered in a seamless
    seal of concrete
that will outlast the fortified roads of Rome
& every single man woman & child shall live in a box by God
the way D. H. Thoreau in his poem Walden said he thought
    they should
all the work will
then be done by
remote
control
machines
& human people do nothing but enjoy such of their superior
    faculties as music appreciation & Understanding Poetry
like this poem of them & America
the very poem they are
the great American national historical automatic personal poem
    without irony or paradox or ambiguity
& the state
will wither away
& expire

It is like field-stripping a forty-five
It is like walking under an occupied gallows without fear
It is like firing up a Dutch Masters President & blowing the smoke
    over some fag's tropical fish tank
It is like reversing the phase of the electric chair circuitry & watching
    the defunct individuals come back to mummy-zombie life
It is light
It is like field-stripping a forty-five in a dark night club
It is like being all pure nose in the moisture of a quiet room full of
    warm nude women
It is like cleaning the portotartarossa instruments of torture with
    pads of steel wool & squares of emery paper & utilizing a new
    whetstone & mill file & applying light-weight machine oil from
    a nice copper can that makes cricket noises
It is like tossing aerosol bombs of flat black enamel into campfires &
    registering a claim for a merit badge in boy scout removal
It is like spit-shining your combat boots with Kiwi black by
    appointment to His Royal Highness that sterling chap the
    Duke of Edinburgh
It is like muffling your dog-tags with friction tape to keep them from
    jangling or reflecting light
It is like waking up in A. D. 802701
It is like putting a forty-five back together blindfolded & sliding in
    the clip until it clicks & releasing the safety & chambering that
    first round
It is like nodding & saying to a bartender Make no mistake
It is like walking in the shadow of an occupied gallows in crepe-soled
    oxfords without gagging
It is like loafing an afternoon away looking at a pretty girl's tongue
    through a big magnifying glass & seeing all the pink taste buds
    there
It is like typing or taping & stapling papers together or punching

holes with a hole-puncher & reinforcing the holes with gummed
reinforcements & attaching paper clips & recruiting your
strength at hydroelectric water fountains with pedals as well as
push buttons where deodorized stenographers display straight
seams & know much shorthand & slip long yellow number-two
pencils through their sprayed hair-do's

It is like meat mother

It is like beating some Desdemona to death with a sweat-sock full of
    wet sand & pulling down the ceiling with a chain & block &
    tackle to make it look like she was accidentally by mistake
    coldcocked in the skull by a falling rafter beam

It is like swallowing slowly at a dirty window watching the passing
    parade panning by like the young nun with venial acne & the
    fat man in mortal Bermuda shorts & the high freaks & janitors
    with goatees & minority groups & snapping their pictures with
    a single-lens-reflex camera

It is like taking a mattock & shovel to dig a deep hole & measuring
    it with a steel tape measure & plumb bob & being pedantic
    about saying digged instead of dug

It is like putting a pit in some sort of earth with occasional insects &
    potsherds & funny peculiar roots

It is like squeezing off twenty rounds from an M-16 set on automatic
    into still water or into the green crown of a coconut tree

It is like the eureka when Max Kiss discovered Ex-Lax in his
    immaculate laboratory

It is like dropping quarter-pound bricks of TNT into the clear water
    offshore thirty feet deep & then cooking some of the resultant
    fish on the beach over a huge fire

It is like running the 120-yard high hurdles in 14.6 then puking
    pizza all over the black cinder track

It is like a hot bath in a Japanese tub with a vodka-tonic in a tall
    glass as big as a tennis-ball can at the tiled edge of the tub &
    a naked nineteen-year-old Japanese lady of exquisite manner
    there while the lime becomes a green light saying Go

It is like the French horn keening throughout Herr Bruckner's
    Fourth Symphony subtitled The Erotic
It is like detail-stripping a forty-five & laying out all the pieces on a
    clean white Cannon Turkish towel placed over your footlocker
    on a Saturday afternoon when everybody else is gone
It is like the famous last words of the Anglican divine who passed
    away saying O death where is thy—
It is like pointing the tube of an eighty-one-millimeter mortar straight
    up at the very zenith & dropping in about twenty rounds before
    the first round comes back down
It is like telling a dog no
It is like saying to the helmsman Left full rudder & All engines
    ahead flank on the bridge of a destroyer of the Fletcher or
    Akikaze class
It is like putting a cigar to the fuze of an M-80 cherry bomb &
    holding it watching the fuze fizz away & bomb go off in your
    paw & spreading on a whole jar of Vaseline petroleum jelly &
    wrapping up the archipelagoes of blood blisters in swaddles of
    cheesecloth
It is like focusing a microscope suddenly to zero in on the spirochetes
    & then turning out the light in a drawing room where there are
    strippers snapping their Beechnut talking to each other &
    putting makeup on their smallpox vaccination scabs & scars
It is like laying the girl next door
It is like slicing carrots with Fulbert's knife & dropping them into a
    saucepan of bubbling boiling tap water
It is like taking action
It is like cutting off your nose
It is like taking action saying to a taxi driver Make no mistake you
    son of a bitch this forty-five is loaded & not with no blanks
It is An Ode Addressed to General Westmoreland on the War

Fellow at the volunteer fire department turkey shoot the other day
    asked me about myself. I told him.
I was brought up by a pack of jackals in Cabarrus County, N. C.
& at the age of eight or thereabouts was found by a farmer who
    sold me to the county seat newspaper The Concord Tribune
which in deadline haste christened me Jackal Girl & named me Ruth
until they burned off my ticks & bathed & barbered me, whereupon
    lo & behold.
I was rechristened Jackal Boy & named William Ruth after old
    number 3 the great Yankee sultan of swat.
Later I added the Harmon from the Herrmannus oldest name in
    Europe carried in the Book of Doom & picked up in Clarissa
    & Our Mutual Friend & Let Us Now Praise Famous Men
& that Thomas Harman whose Caveat or Warning for Common
    Cursetors a forerunner of Red Ryder came out four hundred
    years ago today.
By 1922 I was big in pornography, being the first Golden Superman
    in Havana
& in that same year Miss Stein kindly put me in Geography & Plays
    as a minor character walking on in Act 3 of For the Country
    Entirely where it says

        In the country and for the country.
        Dear Master. Do not say so.
        You mean there is no such address.
        I do not mean that I criticize. I do mean that the
           method used
does not agree with me.
        Certainly not.
          Sincerely yours.
          Harmon.
        Why do you need a name.
        I don't know. I like the point of Inca.

Which last refers obliquely to my savage background.
& even today
forty-five fiscal years later
I still return to my home wilderness from time to time.
Naturally now Ikkihr & Khigghl & Rhononkng-kl-Bniggng XXIII
  & all the other jackals who raised me are dead
but I can still talk the jackal language like a native & remain of
  course a full meat-brother of the pack.
Alas the wilderness of my childhood is becoming less & less free
what with freeways & supermarkets & subdivisions & periodical
  journalism gnawing gnawing
gnawing away at its purity
but it is there yet
& whenever I climb out of my car & strip off my American clothes
  & enter the chaste forest
I am greeted with friendly familiar cries of Auurhnga! Auurhnga!
& know I'm home again

viii

It is an interesting thing this story
in that William you understand equals Wilhelm
Old High German Resolute-Helmet & Defender & Protector
while Harmon is Herman
Old High German again unless I'm mistaken
for Army-Man & Warrior
you see it in Arminius who was Jacob Herman's-son
son of Herman Jacob's-son by the way
& in the middle name of the celebrated Dutch artist Rembrandt
but
& this is important now
note that the middle name is Ruth
which I am told is from the Hebrew for Beauty

& is furthermore an archaic word from the Anglo-Saxon
meaning Pity I believe
but of course I could be entirely wrong

ix

God now I can see what I should of done
(this was years ago now, oh, many moons)

What I should *have* done

Join the circus
Ringling Brothers & Barnum & Bailey
my Pan-American cornet of silver & brass
gone up
like a scalded skylark
above the C above high C
above it all
yes O there
where that one   thin   high   light   silver   line
feels its way step by step over the netless nothing above the Falls
full of barrels full of people
command performance for the King & Queen of England

Join the Redskin Indians (Woollylamb Halfmoon, how)
like in high school we used to talk about
that great tribe of half-assed Indians the
Semi-Holes

Join television
be sad as that poor pitiful beautiful bastard Red Skelton
knocking myself out hour after howling heartbreak hour
Tuesday night for Tide

for a handful of canned laughs
at a time no longer prime
but dumb time
time killed vamping
vamping & waiting for something else to come on

Some*one* else to come on

Join a circle jerk
floating back of some grey filling station at twilight
hand on hand of stump poker with a straight face
or flush face or a bluff & nothing face
not for chips or friends or competitive spirit
but pure joy of the game

Join the Rolls & Royce country club members only
to hobnob with old Saint John O'Hara our Comedian & Martyr

Merchant marine to meet people & hit the beach
with Nelson Algren & Gary Snyder

Join the cannibal Caribbean Isles
drink cowbells with old John Updike
& Herman Wouk & Adam Clayton Powell

Join the grocery to gobble all the red meat raw
on top of blazing catastrophes of pizza pies with pepperoni
& puke in the cash register

In*to* the cash register

Which is a bastard to clean
what with having to get down in there between the keys
& things

Join the damned teamsters
who drive not teams but tractor-trailer trucks
big fucking Macks
with rampant bulldog figureheads
chewing tough George Meany cigars or Red Man

Join politics to make speeches
with a fifty-inch waist
meat people in the YMCA & kiss
babes & get involved in doll-&-dollar scandals
& grin all the while
like a mule eating briars

Join cowboys & get to know old John Ford
Howdy John
nice weather for stealing cows

Join gangsters & get to know Henry Ford
& gun down incomparable Tyrone Power from the back

Join Muslims (William Ruth X)

Join the one true church (William Cardinal Harmon)

Join Confederate Air Force (Kunnel Hah-mun suh) & wear grey
grey
grey everything
to meet people   interesting people
not people like me
with a stopped-up cornet
blowing spit out through the spit-valve
on the floor

On*to* the floor

I am yet the Gross National Product & embrace all things until none is
      trivial
listen to the radio rapt

Life.
      What's that?
A magazine.
      What's it cost?
Ten cents.
      I've only got a nickel.

I am your gross national product & embrace all things
go everywhere—

Attila ruled Huns	Eormanric Goths
Becca Banings	Burgundians Gifica
Caesar ruled Greeks	& Caelic Fins
Hagena Holmrycs	& Heoden Gloms
Witta ruled Swaefs	Wada Selfings
Meaca Myrgings	Mearchealf Hundings
Theodoric ruled Franks	Thyle Rondings
Breoca Brondings	Billing Werns
Oswine ruled Eows	& Yts Gefwulf
Fin Folcwalding	Frisian kind
Sigehere longtime	ruled Sea-Danes
Hnaef Hokings	Helm Wulfings
Saeferth Sycs	Swedes Ongendtheow
Strindberg in Stockholm	another Swede
Sceafthere Ymbers	Sceafa Longbeards
Hun Haetweras	& Holen Wrosns
Herefaras' king	was called Hringweald
Edward the Eighth	for a year in England

Offa ruled Angeln   Alewih Danes
most kaiserly of all   these kings catalogued
yet he over Offa   no sovereignty exercised
for Offa fought   earliest of all
when just a kid   for kingdoms most.
Harmon my father   William Richard
Harmon his father   Charles Richard
his father known   but hardly a Harmon
so grossly am I   a great-grand-bastard
& I was with Huns   & with Hreth-Goths
with Swedes & Geats   & with South Danes
drank beer in Prague   & played much poker
with Wenlas I was & with Waernas   & with vikings
best of men   & boldest boatswains
with Gefthas I was & with Winedas   & with Gefflegas
I was with Angles & Swaefs   & with Aenenas
I fought in France   in forty-four
& in sixty-six   in South Vietnam
with Saxons I was & with Sycgs   & with Sweord-weras
here Harmon had   a hell of a time
with Hrons I was & with Deans   & with Heatho-Reamas
with Thyrings I was   & with Throwends
went abroad on board   the destroyer O'Bannon
& with Burgundians   who gave me this ring
prize-present for poems   a welcome award
(no stingy king, that)   & I might mention
a fat fellowship   from Ford's Foundation
with Franks I was & with Frisians   & with Frumtings
with Rugs & Gloms   & with Rum-Wealhs I was
& I was in Italy   with Aelfwine & (let me see)
in Louisiana also   land of Longs
& Rockefeller running   Little Rock
with Serkings I was   & with Serings
with Greeks I was & with Fins   & with Caesar

who was Führer there   of "felicitous metropolises"
gold & good times   & of Walas' realm
with Scots I was & Picts   & with Scrid-Fins
& drank most deeply   with those dear lords
& tallest tales   were told in cups
with Lid-Vikings & Leons   & with Lombards I was
with Haethens & Haeleths   & Hundings I was
with Israelites I was   & with Ex-Syrings
with Hebrews & Indian Indians   & with Egyptians
who stole my shoes   & all three socks
with Medes & Persians I was   & with Myrgings
("How nice," said the matron: "my mother was a Mead.")
& Mofdings   & again with Myrgings
& with Amothings   with East Thyrings I was & with Eols
who subsist on beer   & barely burned beef
& with Istas   & Idumingas
& I was with Eormanric   Goth king.

Have borne wind-burn   & beat of bad weather
as the sense of space   in a standing creature
facing forward   into its future
lost at velocities   cosmological
the marked red shift   a sign of speed
like "down Doppler"   distancing's index
reflecting itself   in a fall of frequency
as a passing train   drops a quarter tone
so made way among wonders   deeper than waves
among colleges & cannibals   a full career
fixed lance in foes   stranger than fishes
but followed fish too   for the fun thereof
Hethca I sought & Beadeca   & Herelings
in southern hills   home of Harmons
Emerca I sought & Fridla   & East Goth
wise & virtuous   Unwen's father

Secca I sought & Becca   Seafola & Theodric
Heathoric & Sifeca   Hlithe & Incgentheow
Eadwine I sought & Elsa   Aegelmund & Hungar
Wulfhere I sought & Wyrmhere

                              with hard swords
Raedhere I sought & Rondhere   Rumstan & Gislhere
Withergield & Freotheric   & last & not least
Wudga & Hama   of comrades-in-arms by no means the worst

    xi

Deep in the library
built like a dictionary
are vital organs   black lungs
where young men suffer
suffocating among dust books
thick with history   dried-up balls
stone intestines   dense hearts
nuclear kidneys   stomachs perforated
like practice golf balls like collanders
through whose hundred holes pours hot hydrochloric acid
& big wet brains
held red in gleaming jars
wrinkled like piles of spaghetti
with bubbling helical tubes & artillery
of electric arcs & sparks
dramatic in the technical equipment
where young men suffocate almost completely

Almost but not quite
for they catch themselves in time   come to
& use their very last microvolt to escape   rush
out the throat   through the mouth

along the tongue   between the teeth & swinging lips
free at last & rush into the fair fresh air

Partly fresh at any rate
but partly My Sin   garlic   Yardley   farts   DDT   bad dreams
blue True fumes   car monoxide   strontium ninety
cesium one thirty seven   iodine one thirty one SO_x
& thingsome muck that lacks a scientific designation
but scribbles a sort of scorpiony millionaire's X for signature
across black city halls & busted department houses
& fire plugs salted with orange crystals of poodle pee
& the tears old men distil from muscatel

Into fresh air   free
along the straight Chicago sidewalk for instance
an endless wide-gauge stick of chew-gum
through the pedicured well-to-do neighborhood of mansions around
     a lake
which drains at last into a sink-sump swamp of stews & slums
where the gum stick cracks & melts into a protozoon
ooze of dogshit & gluelike involving politics
extending across the almost clean oceans
to bloody places with nasty names like Long Phuoc
where Major Dong obeys Lieutenant Colonel Dung
by administering capital punishment automatically to Corporal Hung
without gagging

Young men partly released from the vines of Marx's big beard
breathing the atmosphere of protest
do not sign their checks with X's
nor move their lips when they read
resist parade weep & get punched out
coldcocked by klansmen maumaus teamsters
Ronald Reagan or waitresses who moonlight wrestling on television

for pin money
& Odorono & Tootsie Roll money & chew-gum dough

— You didn't get that walking into no doorknob young feller
— Yes you're right Doc
I must admit it was a thirty-eight magnum dumdum

& get their curious revolving tongues stuck fast to the trays
in the white frozen food compartment & get their asses flattened on the
      freeway's oceanic heartbeat prosody
& get

& get what?   Nothing
much.   Fucked

   xii

O   the library
bland   harmless & well heated   is being automated
at this terrific rapid clip
by monster RUR & I-be-am Computers
ALGOL gargles into Machine Language bits in that mikrokosmos

Better slip back down that ridged gullet & study steel engravings in
      your grandfather's cyclopedias of phrenology

This shitty air generates a mannered verse
that scans like the mumble of some drunk mother
trying to flush her infant down the commode —
thank god the toilet hasn't worked since god knows when

Ricochet from the library of doctordom to the slum
& react with horror from each then

is to be a pinball rebounding from rubber bumpers
or a thermodynamic pool ball snapping off the cushions
with Left english
or Tarzanoid ball of some sort falling down holes
into sectional intercourse where young men yawn asphyxiating

Be sincere then & tell it straight from the shoulder
holster but offhand like a United States Marine Corps pistol expert
dinging them right down on in there one after the other
at Lejeune or Pendleton or Long Phuoc

ding   ding

Straight
I gross national product say
straight & foursquare
with every inflection from the complex vernacular intact

but with passions from a purer & profounder soul
reaching out to all the random victimized

this first week of the new fiscal year

    xiii

Animals of the forest & plants of the field are friends to me & I
      participate in their organization
I am measured in terms of trillions of dollars
& they understand the nature of husbandry & economy
I walk among the grown-up trees with their attendant vineyard
& rabbits & mice & terrapins are with me in my celebration & with me
      in my deep happiness

O may my blood's truth / still be sung / on this high hill / in a
    fiscal year's turning

xiv

Wind down from the mountains   O from the far west
from the white impure winter born old   to here   the gracious
    eastern spring
that dies young when the summer music comes
& on to the immaculate Atlantic   cold   still cold

Darkness of houses in the winter mountains
Women sit   still & silent   next to tables
dressed in deathly everlastings
Through the short dark days
children look out windows   windows

& (honor the brief lives now) destroyers plunge pitching in Pacific
    typhoons green
steep water up over their bridges breaks & superstructures of
    meaningless aluminum & steel
It laughs at steel & sailors also laugh although they must wash
    much salt from crusted faces
They laugh a lot & tell stories about real storms the way they used
    to be say twenty thirty forty years ago
They laugh on the messdecks when soup spills & food goes flying
    from the pounding table & when they come off four hours
    watch soaked to the skin & tattoos pucker & shirts shrink &
    coffee won't stay in the cup
One makes his way along the deck & is knocked down by a big
    wave like being hit in the breastbone point-blank with a fire
    hose & skids like a fish out of water forty feet along the
    so-called non-skid deck & at the last split second saves himself

from Davy Jones by grabbing a stanchion & holding on tight
with a certain serious dedication
He crawls to his compartment carefully & when they ask him what
    the hell happened he doesn't say death's nether lip just brushed
    his cheek
He says he just lost his God-damned flashlight over the side
& they laugh   devising ways to wedge themselves into their bunks
    for a little snooze without being rocked clean out of the cradle
by old Meat-Mother Pacific & her autumn music

    xv

Crazy the plants put forth smokestacks like the gullets of long guns
& the soot settled like an air of gnats in every eye & smile

hollowed & dried them out & cooked them hard as stone until
they took on that classic colorless knowing look of a skull

O bones not only American men & women but many millions of
    small animals
knocked still in the flooding headlong mindless steeplechase

as if pursued by a madman forest fire screaming from sea to sea
or crazy monster meat creature from another world another earth

    xvi

I'm the Gross National
green thumb & how
my garden grows

I pull suckers from cornstalks
& watch an American toad gobble a likewise American earthworm

with Plato-like detachment

I describe to them the passage in
The Structure of Complex Words
concerning The Bulpington of Blup

I say You toad be G. K. Chesterton
& you stalks be Stephen Duck & H. G. Wells
& you suckers seven times seven types of William Empson

O the sun in its going & going down & going away
covers our great earth
with unutterable beauty

xvii

O bright bomb & circumstance
of intercontinental thermonuclear
up-roar

O what hallelujah of hogs & warships
in the general atmosphere
that downpour day

It is the gross national intercontinental
thermodiplomatic EXEMPLUM
hoo raw

in the which atomic context
talk is cheap
& poems not worth much

But O bright bomb & circumstance

O bride of foreordained tomorrow mornings
& metaphoric mushroom in the blind atomic pilgrimage

Machine language of angels
from zenith to ground
zero

& gross national witness
was there in 1962
during Operation DOMINIC

in the Pacific
around Johnston Island
was there & witnessed

four nuclear explosions
two at midnight & two at dawn
& all four most bloody beautiful

& talk
alas
is cheap

& so
are people
cheap

xviii

Gross & national product sees Washington City capitol & capital
    as paradise with wise men who bear —
George Washington with the Oldsmobile convertible
John Adams with the Orange Crush & Spam sandwich

Thomas Jefferson with the Eskimo Pie
James Madison with the Firestone snow-tire
James Monroe with the Screen Gems Productions
John Quincy Adams with the Arrid under-arm deodorant
Andy Jackson with the Encyclopaedia Americana
Martin Van Buren with the fleet ballistic missile nuclear submarine
William Henry Harrison with the four-deuce mortar
John Tyler with the Trojans
James Knox Polk with the barbecue beef on a bun
Zachary Taylor with the Harz Mountain birdseed
Millard Fillmore with the big bowl of Cheerios for breakfast
Franklin Pierce with the Beechcraft Bonanza
James Buchanan with the Geritol & stack of Decca discs
Abe Lincoln with Ebony
Andrew Johnson with the Hyponex plant food
Ulysses S. Grant with the works of Pearl Buck
Rutherford B. Hayes with the Camel smokes
James A. Garfield with the Michigan State University Marching Band
Chester A. Arthur with the Playtex living bra
Grover Cleveland with the automatic transmission
Benjamin Harrison with the Lennon Sisters
Grover Cleveland with the automatic transmission
William McKinley with the Modern Language Association
Theodore Roosevelt with the installment plan
William Howard Taft with the Wolff Lupus urinal
Woodrow Wilson with the Duncan yo-yo
Warren G. Harding with the Socony Vacuum
Calvin Coolidge with Nancy Sinatra
Herbert C. Hoover with the Daniel Boone Cola
Franklin D. Roosevelt with the Maytag wringer-washer
Harry S Truman with the Birdseye frozen food
Ike Eisenhower with the Smith & Wesson
Jack Kennedy with the Whitman Sampler
Lyndon Johnson with Daisy May Scraggs Yokum

I count all things I witness   I am a teller
The seventh day is not the seventh day because the seventh day is
    the first day
The seventh month is not the seventh month because the seventh
    month is the ninth month
Schubert's seventh symphony is not Schubert's seventh symphony
    because Schubert's seventh symphony is Schubert's ninth
    symphony
Make these lists of things in Saigon   Vung Tau   Cat Lo   Nha Be
    An Thoi   Ha Tien   Phan Thiet   Ham Tan   Cam Ranh
    Qui Nhon   Nha Trang   Da Nang   Bien Hoa   all places I've
    been
gross national product witness & listener & list-maker

xix

William the Teller or Ludibundus Arminius or Trillion Bills the GNP
Uncertified public accountant or radically defeated Catho-Commy
    Coalition candidate for the office of City Chronologer
Semi-pro shortstop until woke up one morning an incurable southpaw
Employee of the circus management or Holder of all pit passes or
    Willy the Penguin (wings to swim with) or double Carolinian
Former senior watch officer or Indian agent or magister artium
    duplex
Arbiter of the barbecue (swineflesh division) or Wart healer
Anonymous author of Standard Operating Procedures for Ships of
    the Fleet Command of the Navy of the Republic of Vietnam
    (Saigon, 1966)
Anonymous co-editor of Public Health Service air-pollution manuals
    Particulate Emission Control & Sulphur Oxide Emission Control
Bat out of hell & loom-fixer general

    O weary reck'ning.

So am I he   the very Mister W. H.
Wm. Harmon twenty-nine years of age in insurable health
going around the world
& noting down the manifest of things

26 December 1961 visited Hiroshima

The catalogue of cities makes a poem of woe a hundred thousand
    hours long
of hunger in the shrunken hearts of the poor & spite in the bloated
    hearts of those no longer poor
& Nagasaki one afternoon in 1962
small glass of brandy in a coffee house
where Beethoven's 9th Symphony was played on a phonograph
& I imitated a haiku of Bashō for a bird-girl
to wit:
        Nagasaki-ya
        aa-Nagasaki-ya
        Nagasaki-ya
which amounts to Nagasaki! Nagasaki! Nagasaki!

October 1964 flew into Gibraltar where the airstrip looks like it's
    too short
& walked around heartbreaking Algeciras all afternoon staring at
    the fascists
rode a dusty bus to Cadiz & had a glass of beer there & flew out
    of Seville a few mornings later absolutely
into the grandest sunrise I ever saw
to Paris & on to London & then on home to Londonderry
& lists of things

Flying home another time Trans-World Airlines 8 February 1967
    from Vietnam
at noon plugged myself into Channel 6 of the Star-Stream Theatre

just as we were catching sight of the great South China Sea
heard in my head Beethoven: Symphony No. 5 in C Minor, Op. 67
    & burst into tears

        xx

poem
is
word
list

a
list
of
words

no
more
no
less

&
vice
versa
:

na
gas
a
ki

like
that

a
ledger
entry

you
do
not
need

to
know
the
key

xxi

> If you don't like my peaches
> why do you shake my tree?
> If you don't like my peaches
> why do you shake my tree?
> Get out of my orchard
> & let my fruit trees be.

Ah

shit.

Hips, hip-sockets, hip-strength, inward & outward
round, man-balls, man-root
not
in the 1st ed. (1855)

Whitman had a dirty mind

In high school we read Leaves of Grass & Venus & Adonis &
    Look Homeward Angel & The Catcher in the Rye for their
    dirty parts
cummings had a dirty mind   Wolfe had a dirty mind   Shakespeare
    had a dirty mind   Chaucer had a very dirty mind
I have a very dirty mind indeed for I have breathed the same air as
    coroners
I have seen coroners' assistants with their stomachs & photographs
ball-headed men in glasses & plastics & synthetics & technical terms
(Ah   shit   in italics)
with stomachs of steel & bone buttons & stills of corpses

I saw one once of a young guy killed in a car crash
He was laid out on his back
Penis & testicles covered up by a little white rectangle

Laurence Sterne & Jonathan Swift & Samuel Richardson had dirty
    minds
Charles Darwin had a dirty mind & thought about shit all the
    God-damn time

& Benjamin Franklin & J. S. Bach & W. B. Yeats & Franklin
    Delano Roosevelt had dirty minds & were foul of mouth
Woodrow Wilson had one of the dirtiest minds in the world

Bloody Lydia Pinkham had a dirtier mind than the worst Lutheran
    convict lying on his left side in his grey cell thinking compulsively
    obsessively about pussy twenty-four hours a day day in day out
    seven days a week fifty-two weeks a year for his entire lifetime
    plus ninety-nine fiscal years for aggravated sodomy & high
    carnal knowledge
& if it's not pussy you can bet it's something even worse

But in the final analysis I think I would have to say that undertakers
    coroners & policemen have the dirtiest minds
& use the foulest language habitually
In high school they told us that the habit-forming use of profane
    obscene vulgar blasphemous language not only stank in the
    nose-drills of Yahweh but also indicated a deficient command of
    the English language
I guess that's right but still have never found a truer clearer or more
    forceful thing to call a son of a bitch than son of a bitch

Sean O'Casey (19 June 1950 Daily Worker): To hell with the atom
    bomb!
But old Allen Ginsberg with his dirty queer dope-fiend commie
    unbusinesslike mind says through his filthy antisocial
    objectionable obnoxious Jewish beard to clean upstanding &
    erect America: Go fuck yourself with your atom bomb.
Now how could that be said better?

"How could that be said better?" a nice old Ulster lady once asked
    me (the text in question being "gem of purest ray serene")
& so I honor her   I really & sincerely do
I honor her here by applying her praise to Ginsberg's scatological
    imperative
Go fuck yourself with your atom bomb

She was born in 1888 named Jane unmarried & my landlady in
    Londonderry
had been a schoolteacher & I don't doubt that she had given a
    great deal of serious thought to the mechanics & logistics of the
    operation of that place in the Miller's Tale where one guy
    gets back at another guy by shoving a red-hot plow-share
    up his ass
O plow & stars
& that reminds me that once when I was out she went into my room

& took my copy of O'Casey's six-volume autobiography &
    later told me that O'Casey was dead that day in Turkey
I could not believe that but she explained (calling me Gorman
    because Harmon is somehow impossible in Gaelic she said)
    that Turkey was a place in Devonshire: Torquay

Ah   man-balls & root
Imagine all the ladies of the temperance & suffragette persuasions
    sitting & sipping bloody Lydia's vegetable compound which was
    one half booze & other half dope
thinking about the body electric & incleft outswell
Zip Zap snap crackle inward & outward round

my ass

   xxii

Now black katzenjammers are shooting up Newark
    (the metal shadow of Krupp slides down the wall
    as the light slides up/
                 a run-thru for the System
               of LeRoi Jones's Hell
    the Krupp diamond slept through Elizabeth's hysterectomy)

blacks shoot up Newark
burning & doing a little looting
while whites shoot up Newark
burning & doing a little looting

pale Hans versus dark Fritz
    Vot der???!!!
              Vass iss?!?!?!?!?!
                        there was the youngster

in old home town Chicago murdered the eight nurses
another young fellow did the Sgt. York routine at the University of
    Texas
    Donnerwetter!!

jawohl jawohl jawohl (click ankles) jawohl mein Führer

This is Niederschlag

vice murders versa all around the planet
Jew murders Arab, Sam murders Janet
you're smart to stay in the ground, Ernest Hemingway — talk about
    your dangerous summers
This ought to qualify

xxiii

Mister Morton Dauwen Zabel he dead
Morton Dauwen Zabel trochaic conveyor belt
& mass production line of flowery platitudes breeding upon platitudes
    platitudes platitude warp & platitude woof & platitudes as far
    as the human eye can see

platitudes about T. S. Eliot
platitudes about Ezra Pound
platitudes about W. B. Yeats
platitudes about W. H. Auden
platitudes about Hart Crane
platitudes about Marianne Moore
platitudes about Wallace Stevens
platitudes about William Carlos Williams
platitudes about Robert Frost

platitudes about E. A. Robinson
platitudes about Robert Bridges
platitudes about G. M. Hopkins
& platitudes about platitudes about Thomas Hardy & Ernest
     Hemingway & Joseph Conrad & Charles Dickens

platitudes up on top of platitudes
granddaddy platitudes to end all platitudes
two platitudes constituting one synoptic platitude
ladders of platitudes & pyramids of platitudes
platitudes on platitudes after platitudes in platitudes
platitudes in Portuguese & platitudes in mannered American English

pair of clandestine platitudes making the platitude with two backs
the platitude of the senior class in the hot house out back making the
     cheerleading platitude next door
begetting baby platitudes arrayed in regimented generations
that flew around the room mewing like bats

thick specs minimized the pupils into idiot points of ignorance lit only
     by momentary gleams of dedicated priggery
& him an editor & critic & teacher of others
& doctor of philosophy & full professor

fullest

But ah well & what the Hell
nil nisi bonum de the dead

let's let it go at that

The world alters every day & cities fall & kingdoms are transferred
for as Petrarch observed we change language habits laws customs
    manners but not vices & not diseases & not the symptoms of
    folly & madness
They are still the same   but of great scenes why speak?
Three summer days I lingered reflecting & even composing *(dichtete)*
    by the Pine-chasms of Vaucluse
& in that clear Lakelet moistened my bread
I have sat under the Palm-trees of Tadmor   smoked a pipe among
    the ruins of Babylon
The great Wall of China I have seen & can testify that it is of grey
    brick & coped & covered with granite
& shows only second-rate masonry

— Great Events, also, have I not witnessed?   Kings sweated down
    (ausgemergelt) into Berlin-&-Milan Customhouse-Officers
The World well won & the World well lost
Oftener than once a hundred-thousand individuals shot (by each
    other) in one day
All kindreds & peoples & nations dashed together & shifted &
    shoveled into heaps that they might ferment there & in time unite
The birthpangs of Democracy wherewith convulsed Europe was
    groaning in cries that reached Heaven could not escape me

Have held converse with the Ultimate Romantic Adolf Hitler in
    Berlin crazy as a bedbug
at the end of his Luger & gasoline & single testicle
the end of one tradition & the beginning of another
up in smoke
            O phoenix Führer
Chaplin & Cleopatra   Giraudoux & Lorca
& the riddle of the body remains unsolved (Police Gazette says he's

in Argentina, but who isn't?)
& have seen little Vietnamese kids line up of a morning to squat on a
    stone fence outside the An Dong Market in Cholon next to
    the Five Oceans Hotel
shitting yellow

O God
(ach Gott)

But last romantics are a dime a dozen
Once or twice I buzzed down the wrong side of a rotten road to Sligo
to wet my loafers in the weeds of Drumcliff Churchyard & check to
    see that Yeats was in the same old place
He was: a mean gravel-covered grave, & that epitaph he specified
I Volkswagenmensch was no horseman but a paid-up member of
    the Automobile Association
& Hitler & Yeats chat in the mind —
& is this your first trip to Germany?   Zo.   What do you think of it?
Does the sun shine this way in Ireland?   I beg your pardon, England?
    I beg your pardon, Constantinople?   Istanbul?   Forgive me,
    forgive me, I mean Byzantium, of course, Byzantium.
Spooks?   Ah . . . no, I can't say that I ever see spooks.   I don't
    even smoke.
I can see them now   neat as nuns   swapping jests   Or Hitler &
    Eliot—
& is this your first trip to Germany?   I see, I see: then you're . . .
    quite zo.   Does the sun shine like this in London?   I beg your
    pardon, Mississippi?   Forgive me, I mean Missouri, of course,
    Missouri.   Poetry?   No, no . . . I never have the time.
    Actually, I don't even eat meat.
& Pound & the Duce have been recorded already (topic: Brazil nuts)

Hell I think I'm the last romantic
& last platonist & thomist & stoic & energist & harmonist &
     antinomian & cynic & epicurean & marxist & puritan &
     federalist & atheist & anarchist & analphabetist

b u t   aaaaaaaaaaaa
please don't lay me away
in a dull yard *mit* weeds in

          xxv

A verse of a Lapland song is haunting my memory still —
from modern Scandinavian languages the expression

                    MEAT-MOTHER

(what peasants call the boss lady)

Loaf-lord & loaf-lady are okay
but that Meat-Mother!

                         must mean metal money
man-money meat-mother

                    my me

Me Crazy Horse
          exclamation point

My chest drum
        I thump bosom
        dried hide head
My chest harp
        I pluck
        yellow wires wow
My chest trombone
        I glide
        the slide boom tink eyow
My chest oboe
        I squeeze
        tears between the reeds eek
My chest old C-melody sax
        I sing songs
        with human voice
My chest Hammond Electric Organ
        I pop stops
        & hide gong
My chest Music Shed at Tanglewood
        I make much music
        money jangle jingle
My chest electronic ether
        I contain canons
        whole radio stations QRM/QRN

xxvi

Bashō's *Zero* dwells in the sun
        hung a moment high above Rimbaud's *Mirage*
& Dryden in a *Spitfire* shoots down the *Messerschmitt* of Goethe
    with his Luger   Iron Cross   the works & so long John

Wars end & now in time of universal peace

Whitman sits at the controls of a *Boeing 707*
TWA made him shave & bring about some changes in his style of life
He has to say Good morning ladies & gentlemen this is your captain
    speaking to welcome you aboard Trans-World's non-stop
    flight to India
If you will look out your window   just to the left   you'll be able to
    see
The long & varied stretch from Puget Sound to Colorado south
Lands bathed in sweeter rarer healthier air   valleys & mountain cliffs
The fields of Nature long prepared & fallow   the silent cyclic
    chemistry
Now we're flying at an alt'tude of two hundred million feet &
    expect to arrive in India right on schedule
It's raining now in India

Star-screwer Ginsberg's the weightless astronaut   high as the quiet
    sky
& in a biplane Faulkner executes history's longest loop-the-loop topped
    off with an Immelman   two Veronicas   & a moonshine toddy
The people clap

His helicopter fell down & the general died
Brave Dengler escaped   survived in the jungle   killed a snake &
    found a rat in the snake's stomach   ate both snake & rat   &
    lived to tell the tale
But the general's helicopter fell to the ground in the mountains &
    burned up
At the Arlington funeral the President kissed the grieving widow's
    cheek

The journey of the fireship is to more than India
& it's raining there too

Europe & Asia   Europe & Asia

                    have I been to
                              Now home   North Carolina   putting it
                              all down
like this very day today   8 o'clock   Friday   21 July   having
    watched my morning TV

New Christy Minstrels: seven gents (white) with sideburns &
    instruments
& two ladies (white) in miniskirts swing & sway away   a wind band
              When those cotton balls get rotten
              You can't pick very much cotton
& the a. m. news is that three hundred Negroes
marched here in Durham County   & one was injured
by a flying object
                        Europe my meat mother
                        Asia my meat mother
                        Africa my meat mother
money America my meat mother
                    When a those a cotton balls git a rotten
                    You can't a pick a very much a cotton
indeed

& they had a men's fashion show (all on the same program)
including a suit of clothes priced at $235   not petty cash

Bread lords: seven nice white guys
meat mommas: two nice white gals down in Louisiana just about a
    mile from Texarkana
You have to watch folksingers folks   I heard a Scotch communist
    group once authentically butcher the Old 97 (wrecked 75 miles
    NW of here)
              It's a mighty long way from Lynchburg to Denver
Yes folks a most mighty long way & most especially so if you leave

Lynchburg & head south   it sure is

        name brands bite size commercials ulcerate lobotomize
& love

Summer of 1954 I wrote to cummings
God knows what muck it must have been but he answered
        as one ignorant human being to another
        i hereby wish you the very best of luck
            Vive la Vie!

& an idle person could spend this July with Life the magazine
the latest of which has a picture story about the young poet
        Berryman's beard & lies about Ireland
(he's a youthful 52 & besides poets run just the reverse of athletes
        who're old men at 30   or Vietnamese whose life expectancy
        is 32)
So here Life gives us a younger poet with a big beard & three wives
        & stories about Irish pubs & how charming the Irish are &
        Ireland is
just like in the Aer Lingus tourist stories
about how green   how green   how green
green friendly   green blarney stone
green sandymount   green dalkey   green gort & cork
green fuck
        Life is my bread-brother in the body of the world of
          money
& television (to quote Washington Alston) my
objective
correlative
        categorical
        imperative

negative
capability

Keep it in perspective

xxvii

Poor Ed Saunders   no sooner had he gotten in good with the
    avant-garde
by writing Poem from Jail & running Fuck You: A Magazine of
    the Arts
than the great money middle-class language machine slapped him
    onto the cover of Life
dot dot dot dot dot dot suppose we last long enough
to need footnotes explaining
meat
explaining Mother

xxviii

Unwelcome news of the gross national day
death of Sandburg in Flat Rock
couple hundred miles west of me here
Flags at half mast today (24 July)
& he so taken with graves & tooooooooooombs
is to be cremated & scattered around Remembrance Rock

So
    lonnnnnnnnng
old
    Carrrrrrrrrrl

Send / us
a post-
        card

& tell
us where
you're staaaaaaaaaaaaaaaaationed

        come on you sons of bitches
        do you want to live forever

The pee-pull
yes the
people

I was a lover of the pee-pull & going to be a communist until it
        developed that Dr. MacDiarmid
had that stand well in hand
& didn't need my help

he lately photographed in Peking
speaking in honour of bag-eyed Blake & vineyard-bearded Whitman
the poster picture of Blake like enough
but the Whitman most unfamiliar until you see that
the Pekinese make old Walt look just like Karl Marx

I happened to be in the "United" "Kingdom" when the doctor
        stood for parliament
it being understood by all & sundry that he would be the communist
        prime minister if his party received a majority

No voter   I made the rounds of public places
with my private face (big eyes, big ears, dish antennas in all
        dimensions)

& number-two pencil   JIM CROW MUST GO   FREE THE
   PRISONERS
NO POPE   & IN MEMORIAM JAMES JOYCE

   xxix

Now
poem & month
both almost over
& done with

riot in Detroit kills three dozen plus
white & black   & Mr. Brown
of the non-student violent disordinating committee
says We built country & we burn it down
& Greece flat under an army dictatorship
Vietnam the same old can of C-ration worms
Red Guards katzenjammer second secretary of Indian embassy
Africa hitting the fan again
Smokey Carbuncle's visiting communist countries
&'s now in Cuba libre swapping jests with the Major
yeh   yeh
            O hot nights & sad days we count you off
witness & tell

                & now John
Coltrane dead

let me put that down
John Coltrane is a dead man

man from Hamlet not far southwest of here

lived forty years of music

impossible music
                              what words what words?
          O long
songs
          Spiritual   Chasin' the Trane   Giant Steps
Cousin Mary   Countdown   Spiral
                              Syeeda's Song Flute   Naima
Mr. P. C.   India   Up 'gainst the Wall
          Impressions
After the Rain   Afro-Blue   The Promise
Alabama   Your Lady   Big Nick

          long songs
let records play

     xxx

          Aaaa-la-ba-ma . . .

Zimmermann Zimmer   Zimmermann Zimmer!

                    when Hölderlin came into the World
                    Kit Smart could die

     200 years ago
& Hölderlin chewed tongue & made poems into letters dated
          100 years in the Future

the muse of meat speaks German in mine ear

Niederschlag   exit Alfried Felix Alwyn Krupp

von Bohlen und Halbach
30 Juli

the prick

xxxi

Uh   say can you see . . .
Uh   beautiful for spacious . . .

          Oh America machinery
that never works perfectly

American meat money machine   each machine
something else   each machine different
as each rose or dollar is another thing

All looms & rudders bind up
as the grey goose broke the hog's teeth out
broke the saw's teeth out
                    story Hawthorne mentioned
sung by Leadbelly
of hog & saw the teeth broken

Gre't day in th' mornin'!   Balls o' far!

Each machine language operates idiosyncratically imperfectly
whereof is developed the beauty & the flower-poetry

Imagine each machine
       singing its song
particular   peculiar

Looms & radars hum or sing aloud
                              Eliot & Leadbelly mumbling

Machined birds
con el sexo atravesado
por una aguja
                    penis needled for the meat-mother
& money mad machine

        the beauty of the mint
        & glory of the mint museum

        Uh   American man can

        & I —

My body is the landscape & the song

        incorporating

My fantastic interstate highways
        leaping like salmon upward to New York holy city
        shot like shuttles across the dancing warp
& narrow no-count farm-to-market roads with not even a white line
        down the middle

The loom graph is laid down in the two dimensions

I am the dance of the graph across the loom warp

ch'êng!   chng —— chng!   it∫ən!

The dance is a song with words & the words are dirt & the body money

Explicit metaphors are unnecessary

I incorporate gullies full of rusting beer cans   both the poptop &
    those requiring a church-key   thrown at night from fast happy
    bloodmobiles

In the wild old days we drank quarts of Bud & pissed on tombstones
    in a cemetery near a country church   I have always rather
    regretted that
O quarts of Pabst or Blatz or Schlitz   or in a pinch Primo of Hawaii
    or Atlantic of Carolina the cheapest beer
& pissed my whole name on a dirt road someplace

Hendecasyllabic anacolutha are not worth the sweating

Screw terza rima
Screw terza rima
Screw terza rima

                  Hand me my random-lead cam

xxxii

                           31 July
So let the month end   the new fiscal year
is well underway with way on

The earth machine is falling or flying apart like usual
(old man saw his first locomotive & said They'll never get it started —
when they got it started with a roar of sparks he said They'll never
    get it stopped)

I plan my television afternoon

Channel 5 – MOVIE – Drama
    "The Garden of Allah." (1936) A Trappist monk runs away to
    the desert where he meets a beautiful woman who has gone
    there to find peace.   Marlene Dietrich, Charles Boyer.

Sounds okay. & tonight, also on 5

    "Salty O'Rourke." (1945) A gambler who is readying his horse
    for an important race falls in love with a pretty teacher. Alan
    Ladd, Gail Russell.

Sphaera cuius centrum ubique, circumferentia nullibi   until signoff
    with the national ditty unsingable
& shots of troops smartly lined up with Springfields at present-arms
    & stars & stripes floating in the breath from paradise

Picture clicked off   collapsing   shrinks to a single self-centered
    bright infolding point
imploding star of light   light years off & then disappears quite
into the heart of the mother

madmoder   *madmoder*   *madmoder*

meat mother muse money machine motor metal man me
    madmoder

xxxiii

Flying home from Vietnam across thirteen time-zones
I underwent an 8 February thirty-seven hours long
& read O'Casey's autobiography chapter "A Long Ashwednesday"

With such a cross of Camel ash between my eyes watched
    "The Garden of Allah"
Trappist & lady with eyes the size of tennis balls & number-two
    eyebrows honeymooning on the all-proving desert ground
with a handkerchief-headed Basil Rathbone (who just died)

The present past in the plastic box with glass & the cathode ray
    back to 1936
year of the death of Lorca
                 —antennae are the poets of the race

by means of needles
 Boyer & Mar(ia Magda)lene
            by means of Needles

Mystery of the body never solved/
               limbo
by means of electric needles
on just such
a summer's day

means of needles in just such a month of July

      leaves of plastic
          flowers of plastic

First month
of the happy
fiscal year

the wilderness of Spain & politics

in the lap of the blood of the mother's meat

                    past all Calculation & belief it Came so huge
What colored cartoon Rodent could antimatter nightmare or
     imagine It
A carrot Carrot growing wilde O Carrot wildly wildly
& bloody huge too over Polite city's placid nursing Landscape's
     blah horizon
It came from Saturn's purgatory Ring
It came from Ataulfus king of the visigoths Assassinated at
     Barcelona in 415
It came from Mercury the winter Camp of Jesus trismegistus
From Peter pumpkin eater & Unkulunkulu
It came from the Home of the free recognizing F. Franco on the
     day of Fools in april 1939
It came from half-unlit Pee-green halls of Halitosis muscatel
     Salvation & used sheiks that made light love Safe for
     Deomoncratz & guildenstern
It came I tell you from tecumseh & Tenskwatawa & Tashunca-uitco
From 1813 from 1834 & 1877
& from the poet prophet Priest Nezahualcoyotl forging Prescriptions
     for terpin hydrate Elixir & Q-Tips & C-quens on red & Green
     gift-wrapping Paper in the lost Linen Closet of an Oddfellows
     Hall in 1520 with Luther excommunicated by Leo X &
     Raphael & Montezuma II dead
It came from the Human Mind of Man & the Rosy burning Sled
     of xanadu & Its majesty the Rann of kutch
From Bird's milk & Celery Stalks at midnight & Hide Pock &
     Afrika Korps & Eric's popskull burden
It came from Hubert Hubert Hubert & the deterministic Ur-stratum
     of Quantum phenomena & the Belles of birmingham memorizing
     Gin
It came from those lordly king Solomon's orchids the 10 educated
     toes in Stalin's burial socks

It came from 1953 & the Girl Next Door
From Arnold Bax & pepsic Ulcers & the death of Scanderbeg
    the albanian chief in 1468
It came from Berg his concerto for Violin & orchestra
& from Pavane pour une Infante défunte & the kinderTotenlieder
It came I say from 1935 & 1902 & 1899
From mux duRatt & young Lester leaping in & Supermarket
    Sweepings & the Edoo variation
It came from Michelangelo's statue of Malcolm x dying a Sunday
    & K K K Katy
It came from Nebuchadrezzar in Jerusalem in 588 b. C.
It came from Jacqueline's ruby queene pressed between the Papers
    of the Yellow pages in Euclid in Ohio o god
From aldershot Principia & Plutonius XC & the Trillion Elizabeth
    asylum electricities
It came from Phatic communion & ethnical culture & Korsakov's
    Syndrome & Anal-sadistic pseudonames & All the 1960's
From supersuds & the hysterical East following a sternstar &
    bran-clean from Engine Love call & the hi-freak stainless-Gold
    antennae of Troy VIIA's DonaHue hairs in 1184 B. C.
It came a long Way from Saint Francis
It came Express collect Emergency from the mood music of
    Cosmo McMoon & from Tapoti—to the Melody of P'u Sa Man
    written after the 4th Encirclement in February 1933
It came from Pink Pills for Pale People & The Blues To End All
    Blues & Oscar Boom (Wonmug is Einstein) & farcing
    Milky Ways & Baby ruths & from the Universal International
    harvester His Self
& from Aix-les-bains & algernon Bray & ARVN & cheeky Bob &
    Bradshaw of the Future & B. Suárez Lynch on 24 May 1881
    the astronomically most Beautiful easter in the memory of
    Man kind
From J. J. Fux & Bust her Brown & remote control Cola's Norbert
    the Wiener & the megapolice of Babeloan & Steam Rose Beret

It came from Edgar à Perry & Silas Tomkyn Comberbacke on
　　2 December 1793 & Mary midnight & Mister Lun & zosimus
　　zephyr & ferdinando's Foot & Billy the Lip & Ebenezer
　　Cardinal Pentweazle & Martinus Macularius & Quibus Flestrin
　　& the Female student & Mark & judy Twain
It came from bloomfountain of Vesuvius petroleum Dow & New
　　South Wails & the Briddish crown colon of Watt in california
　　& The Hekiganroku a a
Came riding tall sidesaddle on the back of a Limerick Pig of steel
　　wearing this long & flowing Dirty white robe with Magic
　　marker scenes of the Rape of Antarctica
It came to Me my melancholy Baby drinks too much & gruen Ticks
O it came from a Rose
It came from a Yes
It came from the Automon Umpyre & Sow-Jet union castronuts &
　　Metacomet cleanser & Lifey's butter dream of Detroit barbecue
　　Ritz with the Blue Lights On
It came from Nahum & the Dried-up Lips of mister Cornelius
　　McGillicuddy of the old Philadolphia athaletics Basebol
　　organization
It tame tause see im a dood dallar in odle sings　iss & so im Dd too
　　Gd bless MD & FW & Me　ay & pdfr too　farewell MD MD
　　MD FW FW FW Me Me
Came from the Top & Vo nguyen Giap & the Dalkey archive &
　　Engelbeng humperdumbp & simon gerfalcon & Tender Loins
　　& the Mom of Golly
It came leaping blubber lubber from the Innard slick perkeo of
　　Moby Finn
From fitch shampoo & billiard Greens & Moon of the Mullins
Is come from the Sixtieth chapter of the Book of Isaiah & Smoking
　　flax the Toothsome Eel of the Wabash & P. P. Bliss & all
　　God's Chalk
It came from Johannes de Silentio copenhagen 1843 & V. Dixon &

Macapagal in Malacañang & 2-way Inventions for simulated
    Limousine & Yokum fun Ribbentrop in F-cup Major
It came from all future Prolegomena & anathemata & the Land of
    Moles & Pismires & hammer headed Hobbes
From I say Teapot Dome wyoming & That crowd of aristocrats
    our betters fornicating their Monocles & orders off in the pule
    at Cliveden & in the weeping stoneflint waters of the Pedernales
    a River in Hell
It came from Oppenheimer seeing sanskrit in the A-boom blossom
    & Wild turkey drink with Quail Roost Noble Primrose of the
    Mûng sisters
It came from Tennessee Ernie & the San kenton quhair doing
    A Mighty fortress
It came one uncertain April day with Operation PLUTO defunct in
    Pigs' Bay & from blonded Bomb shells dead in bed of Ovadoses
    of Selleuloid & from the Eightfold quark of mann
From the protocols of Dayan & wonderings of Ossian & deficit
    Spending & the Lysol Gap & Voronoff money glands & minus
    fours & Jackson Pollock's unimagineable cowhand Genius
    pissing back & Forth & round & round in Miss Peggy's
    gugenheim Fire & the Field of the Cloth of Gold
It came about ten Thousand Years ago from the follicles of
    Montgomery sutra & red squares & the Shankletown strutters'
    Prince of denmark March
From Kitchen Sink & new Maximico Time's picayune & the Great
    Speckle Odes
It came mad from Cro-magnon Adam man & Woman in cool
    Booth of Musak shopping sinner cock-tail Lounge open 24
    hours the day by molotov no cover no minimum no limit until
    the Cops came & Locke came
It came I was Alone I should have known
& it came to pass Moroni was angry with the Govt. because of their
    Indifference concerning the Freedom of their Country about
    B. C. 62

It came a-frugging from the Forbidden City of honolulu Burlesque
  O god in heaven All Mighty that naked woman music &
  jazz-physics There
From biograph & Ford & Texas Theatre & hurry Davidson & the
  Crédit mobilier of Americard & Star & Garter Chambers &
  the Gross National Manifest destiny
It came from Finnegans final Fall & all & mikrokosmos
  Hellzapoppin Götterdämmerung & sump
It came from them
        Him me you
        O go down
        On our
        Knees
        now